HEALING HEALS THE HEALER TOO

David Sauvage

Copyright © 2020 by David Sauvage

Cover design by Ivan Kurylenko

This book is typeset in Unna

Designed By Hannah Gaskamp

ISBN: 979-864723-858-0 (paperback)

Printed In The United States Of America
20 21 22 23 24 25 26 27 28 / 9 8 7 6 5 4 3 2 1

*For David Solie,
who believed in me.*

Table of Contents

9	Introduction
11	Don't Kill Yourself over a Resume
12	Why We're Here on Earth
13	The Psychic Taxi Cab
14	Trump
15	To My Friends Blessed with Wealth
16	Intuitive Readings as Performance Art
17	To All the Depressives and Neurotics
18	The Tao
19	The Pain of Being Broke
20	My Twenty-Year High School Reunion
21	Fuck Effort
22	Now Is the Time to Heal
23	What I Needed to Hear When I Was Suicidal
24	Why People Don't Help More
25	Many Brave and Beautiful Souls Are Doing Good but Not Doing Well
27	Why Do I Want to Be Better Than I Am?
28	The Healer
29	Trauma and the Personality
30	How I Confused Money and Love
31	Our Full and Broken Hearts

32	I've Been Desperate for Decades
34	Thank God for Burning Man
35	Occupy Wall Street
37	Charles Eisenstein Enlightens Me
39	My Friend Pamela Faces Death
41	5-MeO-DMT
43	My Intention for My Ayahuasca Ceremony
45	The Ceremony
48	Healing Intergenerational Trauma
50	It's Not About the Money
52	The Right Person Is the One Who Is Called
53	All Emotions Are Okay
54	If Enough of Us...
55	It's Time to Wake Up
56	My New Year's Resolution
57	The Greatest News No One Ever Shared with Me
58	A Gift from a Stranger
59	It's Okay to Be Numb
60	How to Liberate Yourself
61	Spiritual Growth Tip #273
62	What I Really Want
63	Why I Went to Burning Man Even Though I Didn't Really Want To
66	Why Almost No One Takes Responsibility
67	The Big Lie We All Swallowed

68	I Recommend Developing an Internal Sense of Self
69	Premium Class
70	Is This the Awakening?
72	The Dark Force Threatening to Destroy Us All
73	Are We Ready?
74	We're Almost There
75	Goodbye, Bernie
77	We Do Not Have to Be Productive. We Do Not Have to Be Productive. We Do Not Have to Be Productive.
79	Afterword
81	Acknowledgements

Introduction

This book is a collection of Facebook posts I wrote from 2013 to early 2020. I'm a touch self-conscious about presenting them as a book, because they were Facebook posts after all, and Facebook posts aren't a book. But a deep impulse had me read them over. Another deep impulse had me send them to my friend Faye, who's an editor. The more Faye and I worked at it, the more it felt like it was worth doing.

The posts are about deep healing, psychedelics, Burning Man, radical politics, money, psychic abilities, the absurd standards our insane culture holds us to, and the need for community. If these subjects interest you, I think you'll enjoy the read. But the real thing going on here is an authentic and sincere expression of my beliefs and feelings. I hope they resonate. More than resonate; I hope they move you. I hope they open your heart. I hope they're healing.

The posts are chronological. I grow and mature as you go along. There's a story here, if you'd like to track it, but I don't mind one bit if you skip around. Feel free to pick a title that excites you and jump right in. I love reading books that way, in little bites. I'm remembering those now obscure but once famous collections of essays by Montaigne or, better yet, Schopenhauer, that I devoured as a teenager.

Here's a little about me. I'm writing these words in my East Village apartment in New York City. Picture a curly-haired Jewish fellow, 39 years old and single, ordering takeout in the midst of the pandemic. Until a few years ago, I was making a living, not a particularly good one, directing commercials for brands like BMW and Sprint while trying and failing to get documentary films financed. I left the film business, or the film business left me, and I became something of a healer.

My gift is the ability to feel what other people are feeling. In other words, I'm an empath. You could say I turned this gift into a career, but the truth is, the gift grabbed ahold of me and wouldn't let go. I use my intuition to help people process their emotions and find answers to the big questions in their lives.

I also do performance art. Pre-virus, you might have found me on stage, doing intuitive readings in front of audiences. I ask for a volunteer, take their hand, allow their emotions into my body, and express what I feel they're feeling. I'm not 100% accurate, but accuracy isn't the point. I'm demonstrating that empathy is a real-life superpower. And that we're more connected than we imagine.

I've gone on quite a journey from frustrated filmmaker to embodied empath. These are the truths I found along the way.

MAY 19, 2020
NEW YORK CITY

Don't Kill Yourself over a Resume

This past Monday night, on the subway platform, a young man sat down on the edge, his legs dangling over the side, just five feet from me. "You probably don't want to do that," I said.

He pivoted around, tears in his eyes. "I don't know... my resume..." he said.

"I'm sure you can fix the resume problem in another way," I said.

He got up, stumbled over to me, drunk, and sat down. We chatted for the next twenty minutes about suicide, what it means to struggle, and why it was better to wait things out, especially when you're 26. I offered to see him home, but he shook his head. Then he thanked me and got on the train. I hope he's okay.

OCTOBER 2, 2013

Why We're Here on Earth

There is a human story all of us live. There is also an economic one. They will inevitably come into conflict. One major test of our character, in this age and time, is whether we serve others and try to make money in the meanwhile, or whether we serve money and try merely not to hurt people. We can't have been put on Earth for the money, but we may very well have been put on Earth for each other.

MARCH 24, 2014

The Psychic Taxi Cab

Trekking back from Burning Man with my hair all dusty and my throat all scratchy, I feel sad. I hand over five bucks for a falafel, and the exchange is pleasant but flat. At Burning Man, there was not a dollar exchanged. The only currencies were gifts and gratitude.

For a few years now, I've been aware of, though sometimes afraid to acknowledge, my empathic abilities. I can feel people's feelings at will. Not just their feelings right now, but their emotional state overall, their anxieties, joys, hopes, and fears, sometimes to surreal specificity. It took Burning Man and its culture of giving to give me the courage to take a piece of cardboard over to the airbrush booth and ask the artist to write PSYCHIC READINGS in bold, flowing black. On the corner of 9:30 and E, I parked my bike at a wooden carriage dubbed by its caretakers "The Psychic Taxi Cab" and introduced myself as the new resident psychic. Over the next three days, thirty or forty people sat down in front of me. I took their hands, closed my eyes, and spoke what I felt and saw.

I knew I had this ability, but this was the first time I could give it, to one person after another, in a way that felt a part of me rather than a gimmick, a response to a dare, or as evidence against a skeptic. The gift you bring, which might otherwise be dismissed as a hobby or an interest or an idle passion, is as essential at Burning Man as your bike and your LED lights. It's awesome.

SEPTEMBER 8, 2015

Trump

Trump is our country's shadow, the darkest part of ourselves. The only way to mature past the shadow is to acknowledge and integrate it. Clinton represented the lie that we could meet suffering and rage with centrism and superiority. No. We have to go deeper, take the long walk down into our own truth, and start again with an honest engagement with reality, the horrors we have been perpetrating on the world and each other, the smugness, the derision... And on the other side, we become our better self. Our true self.

NOVEMBER 12, 2016

To My Friends Blessed with Wealth

The shift will be upon us when hundreds of millions of dollars start flowing toward transformational change, rather than merely alleviating the problems of the current system, without any consideration of returns. I know so many artists, activists, and visionaries who are giving 100% of themselves to this new world, but I have yet to hear a story of a philanthropist going all in to create what we all sense we need.

To my friends blessed with wealth: the world is calling for you. It's calling for you to give from your heart, for the creation of something deeply true to you, a creation not born of guilt, not extracted from you by fundraisers, not proven to you with spreadsheets. It is beyond the measurement of impact and well beyond impact investing. It is the art of your soul, made real through money, a force that moves through you and that you are ready, now, to heed.

Thank you in advance from the future. We are all grateful.

OCTOBER 1, 2017

Intuitive Readings as Performance Art

Three nights in a row, I sat in a chair at the ABXY Gallery on the Lower East Side and did intuitive readings as a kind of performance art. Whoever wanted could sit in the chair across from me. I closed my eyes, took their hand, and felt their emotions. Then I expressed, physically and verbally, what I felt they were feeling, in front of audiences that ranged from 0 to 100 people.

Sometimes I nailed it, sometimes I fumbled, sometimes it was exquisite, and sometimes it was exquisitely awkward. I felt every kind of emotion in others, familiar ones with names we know, like sadness and anger and joy and wonder, and less familiar ones and harder to name ones, like "a vulnerable kind of feminine bliss" or "the kind of disgust that can turn into resentment" or "a heavy blanket that covers you."

My art was to express the part of me that doesn't even exist, to express the emptiness that is at my center, emerging through the thin veneer of my personality, this newly light-hearted but generally ironic man that is me. And I feel like saying, I did it. I actually did it.

OCTOBER 18, 2017

To All the Depressives and Neurotics

As I work on my play "Empath," I am struck by how little I ever shared of my sadness, depression, and suicidal urges which consumed so much of my twenties and early thirties. Now that I am no longer depressed, now that I have direction and moments (or days!) of happiness, it feels safe to talk about it, even publicize it. That is our culture: we celebrate success, celebrate growth, celebrate coming out on the other side, but we abandon and problematize the millions and billions of people suffering deeply right now, trapped between the big lie that they ought to figure it out on their own and the belief that they are helpless.

To all the depressives contemplating suicide, to the neurotics suffocating with anxiety, to the victims lost in the story of their own victimhood, let me tell you this: it's not about hoping for a better future, it's not about transcending your circumstances or remaking yourself or doing deep healing and emerging whole one day, it's not about getting over yourself or doing something with your life or helping others or finding God or getting a job or eating better or meditating consistently. Allow yourself to take all the condescending "We know what's wrong with you" advice and dump it into the abyss. And instead, play with this idea, if you want (and if you don't want, don't; who the hell am I?): you are a human being right now, you are having an experience of life right now, and your experience is true and real and raw and deep. And we—all the people doing well enough to post happy pics on Instagram—owe you an acknowledgement. Your story is true, too. Share it if you want to.

MARCH 1, 2018

The Tao

Imagine for one moment. You weren't doing it for money. Or to get ahead. Or to make sure someone important noticed. Or because you felt guilty, like you should do it. Or because it's what you've done so you're used to it. Or because you had to do it, because obviously. Imagine for one moment you did it because it was you, just you, doing.

APRIL 4, 2018

The Pain of Being Broke

Over ten days in my silent retreat, the issue that kept coming up for me was money. It has been a major source of pain over the last 15 years. When I followed my heart, I rarely earned enough to cover my basic lifestyle. When I tried, sometimes desperately, to do what would make money, I found life gray and hopeless and could neither make money nor find joy. Debt resulted, on top of student loans, and so much shame and embarrassment. I asked friends for help. Most of them gave a cold assessment of my skills and got to work trying to plug me into the matrix. "Suck it up," they said. My heart closed and my energy evaporated. Others encouraged me to keep going and promised it would be fine. It was not fine.

Only a few days ago, in pure silence, did it occur to me: I had never tried being kind to myself in this struggle, never acknowledged this struggle to myself as legitimate and overwhelming, never held my own pain through years of credit card debt and couch surfing and crushing rejections from financiers saying that while what I was selling was great, it wasn't commercial enough. No one ever sat with me in my desperation and showed compassion for it. And finally I realized I needed to sit with myself there first. Or to put it more plainly, I need to sit with myself in the here and now. I am in difficult financial straits. But I have a pure heart, the courage to stand in my truth, and talents that blow people away. I am okay as I am. And it's okay that it hurts.

MAY 7, 2018

My Twenty-Year High School Reunion

Headed to my twenty-year high school reunion, it occurs to me that I've achieved nothing I'd hoped for. I haven't made a feature film let alone succeeded as a filmmaker, haven't made a bunch of money, haven't gotten married or had kids. And yet I've achieved so much more than I imagined. I went to my darkest parts, opened them up, and moved through them; I survived years of suicidal thoughts to emerge whole and present; and I have expressed myself honestly on stage and page and screen. So I have these feelings of inadequacy, of failing, but then again, I remind myself, I've done a lot.

MAY 19, 2018

Fuck Effort

Recently I've been playing with the idea that I don't have to do anything that doesn't feel true to me, even if it appears logical that I have to do it. As I describe this radical approach, I've noticed it upsets a lot of people, who are prone to call me anything from entitled to lazy to naive to self-sabotaging. We are so brainwashed into the idea that success comes from suffering, that work has to be hard, that we just have to will ourselves to greatness through discipline and focus, when I'm discovering the exact opposite is true. My success is coming from what is most joyful; my greatest work is often my easiest; and I have absolutely had it with the notion that the realization of my dreams is hiding on the other side of tons and tons of effort. Consider that our system is so broken (and so clever) that it tricks us into believing that we have to fix ourselves when we should be banding together and declaring ENOUGH. What might happen if we resisted just by allowing ourselves to be as we are? And what if enough of us did it together?

MAY 25, 2018

Now Is the Time to Heal

Whatever it is, it appears to be happening, at least in the communities I know. We are finding it harder and harder to kid ourselves that just because something makes money, it's good; or just because someone will pay us to do it, it's fine; or just because everyone else is doing it, no worries. The universal, semi-conscious conscience is asserting itself more and more. Feel it yourself as a pull toward purpose or toward the heart, not in some cheesy just-talk-about-it-but-do-nothing kind of way, but more like: Wait a second, I'm alive on a burning planet, I've got gifts or wealth or time or radiance to spare, and I need to use it, for real, right now. Or even more powerfully: I'm broken or hurting or anxious or depressed, and it's blocking me from my full expression. It's time to heal. Yes, yes, now.

JUNE 3, 2018

What I Needed to Hear When I Was Suicidal

I'm doing really well now, but I had years of playing with, fantasizing about, and occasionally planning suicide. What I think I needed to hear most, which no one told me, was that it was okay to want to die, that wanting to die was a natural symptom of deep suffering, that there was no easy solution, and that the pain I was in was real, serious, and worthy of care, even if no one I knew could deal with it. Nowadays, I feel good, even happy. And those are the words I told myself that helped get me here.

JUNE 10, 2018

Why People Don't Help More

My friend Pamela reminded me that this national conversation on suicide inevitably points to the question, "Why don't people help more?" It's not enough to say to those wanting to die that they can or should ask for help. Sometimes asking for help generates *more* pain, because pleas are rejected or trivialized. During my suicidal periods, the most common response I got, when I vocalized whatever aspect of my suffering I mustered the courage to share, was to get a job. Second to that was to get on antidepressants. Both responses drove me further down the rabbit hole.

    I believe people care. We care about our fellow humans. But we do not know how to listen to, appreciate, or honestly engage with the emotional experiences of others. They scare the hell out of us. And that is because we don't know how to do it for ourselves. Do you welcome and hold dear your own pain, or do you tell yourself to suck it up? Do you attend to your loneliness with compassion, or do you distract yourself with media? These habits run deep, and they magnify themselves when we encounter people suffering even more deeply. I can hold space for others to the exact degree that I can hold space for myself. I can sit with someone who wants to die because I can sit with myself there too. If you want to be present for another, be present for yourself, and it will follow naturally.

JUNE 10, 2018

Many Brave and Beautiful Souls Are Doing Good but Not Doing Well

I sense my money woes are coming to an end. People are paying me to do things that light me up. I notice, though, that this breakthrough follows years of unpaid work done in silence, years I financed with credit card debt and loans, years of painful introspection and plant medicine and writing stuff no one will ever read. And during those years, I carried the belief that I was doing something wrong because I wasn't making money. I was told countless times that I wasn't disciplined enough. Or that I needed to get over myself and play the game. Or worst of all, most painful of all, that my attitude, or my belief system, was the problem.

The idea is common in spiritual circles, and to my mind, it's toxic: If you align with your highest purpose, spiritual types will tell you, abundance follows. Sure, maybe, after years. Or maybe not. Maybe never. Not to mention the countless millionaires who are disconnected from themselves and their hearts. If there really is some magical secret money formula beyond just selling your skills in the marketplace, being born into the right family, or investing in Bitcoin two years ago, let's have compassion for those of us who never learned it. And let's work for a world where every single human being, no matter how comfortable they are with the word "abundance," has the resources they need to express their full potential.

There may be a way to "do well by doing good," but there are so many brave and beautiful souls doing good and not doing well. I see you. I believe in you. You may be doing exactly what's needed for this planet right now. Or for yourself. And you count too.

JUNE 17, 2018

Why Do I Want to Be Better Than I Am?

I woke up, I told myself I should go to the gym, I told myself I should journal. Instead I checked Facebook, watched Sweden beat Mexico, and felt guilty about it. An old pattern: to hold myself to some standard of productivity, or even of self-care; to compare myself to another, hypothetical David, one who wakes up, meditates, kills it at the gym, and super-focuses on the tasks at hand. But why is this David better than the real one? Who decides these things? Who told me I was irresponsible and lazy, and why do I listen?

It's okay to want to be more than you are. But whatever you're trying to be more of, it's worth asking where that standard came from. Maybe the "more" to aspire to is just more self-accepting and more self-loving.

JUNE 27, 2018

The Healer

Healing heals the healer too.

JULY 1, 2018

Trauma and the Personality

Personality, I'm discovering, is an awkward compromise between who we really are and who we believe we must be to be loved. What looks like someone's personality is, more often than not, a deeply embedded pattern of reactions to unprocessed, often multi-generational, traumas. As we process the traumas, the personality shifts and lightens, and what takes its place is an emptier essence meant for experiences and gifts to flow through.

JULY 8, 2018

How I Confused Money and Love

I have been digging deeper, ever deeper, into my relationship with money—the cycle of debt and martyrdom (and some might say entitlement) that has come with following my deepest intuition. What occurred to me after yet another weekend of ayahuasca, puking, holding space for the trauma of others, and feeling the pain of multiple men who had beaten themselves into successful careers when they actually needed the gentle love of women, was that I had conflated money with love.

When people give me money, not for doing something for them but for being who I truly am, I feel the warmth and support of unconditional love. But when people pay me to serve their goals rather than their souls, I feel used. I simply can't tolerate anymore that subtle feeling of dehumanization that comes with surrendering the self to please someone who's paying, that little lie in our intonation that salespeople use to put someone who's powerful at ease with their made-up reality. So I am forced to stand up and argue for a world where we can all be free to be ourselves, where we get food and shelter and love because we matter as humans, not because we can afford it. This is my psychology, whether I like it or not. I'm starting to like it.

AUGUST 8, 2018

Our Full and Broken Hearts

One of the great revelations of my life is that I actually need to process the pain of rejection rather than suck it up. For about ten years, I brought project after project to Hollywood's altar, and every one was rejected by networks and studios. When I complained or lamented, I was told to get over myself, that it came with the territory, that if I wanted a career in this business I had better get used to it. In retrospect, this was terrible advice, albeit common. What I needed to hear was that it was okay that it hurt each time, that I needed to take care of myself through the pain, and that it wasn't so much my ideas or my vision that was the problem, but a media ecosystem (and a society as a whole) that values profit, status, and distraction over quality, meaning, and truth.

In the last month, two production companies passed on a show about my work, and I fell into the same old pattern: blaming myself for being rejected, blaming myself for caring so much, and shutting down as if what I was doing would never be enough for "them." But this time, I see the pattern. And I tell myself I can fall apart all I want and feel as badly as I want. It really isn't me. Or any of us. It's a great big machine that teaches us in a thousand different ways that we don't matter. But we do.

It's not our job to suck it up. It's our job to feel the pain. To feel every last bit of it. So we can know how bad it hurts. So we can change the whole thing with our full and broken hearts.

AUGUST 12, 2018

I've Been Desperate for Decades

I have been enjoying, really enjoying, posting vulnerable, awkward thoughts and feelings around money, Hollywood, depression, and the cruelty of our economic system. One of the pieces of feedback I get, or I can feel from people, is the sense that I seem "desperate." And that this desperation is "unattractive." Desperation is one of those qualities in people we find most repulsive, unless it's in a charged sexual context—but otherwise, keep away. We have been taught to keep our desperation to ourselves, as it's shameful to admit so much lack. Or worse, we've been told that all we need to do is believe in abundance, or let go of our attachments, or give ourselves enough self-love, and POOF, all that desperation goes away. No, no, no. Desperation is a real feeling, deeply felt by most people, hiding behind mists of shame and pretense. I have been desperate for decades—desperate for validation of my gifts and even more desperate for a sense of belonging in a culture that tells me (not in words, but in how it apportions resources) that I do not belong. I am less and less desperate now, and now it feels safe to talk about it. And I can tell you, offering myself as proof, that it does go away, like any emotion, when you get to know it, when you listen to it and acknowledge it and honor it. And as it goes away in me, I feel so much compassion, so much, for all the desperate humans out there who do not yet have the ability, or the courage, or the awareness, or the safe spaces they need to share their desperation. Can we be desperate together? Desperate for belonging, for community, for intimacy, for purpose? And can we address, or work toward addressing, truly and honestly and finally, our deepest unmet needs? The fictions are dissolving, the mists are lifting, and from my clear vantage point I can say one thing with certainty: we need each other.

AUGUST 14, 2018

Thank God for Burning Man

If there's one thing I'll take from my second go-round at Black Rock City, it's how fleeting this whole game of life is. As the Man burns, I sense how little power we have to shift the ultimate course of events, how trivial the tiny turns of our experience are in the Grand Scheme of Things, and how goddamn glorious it can be to embrace the now, to embrace it with our bodies and beings, to shed, through the sheer power of overwhelm (and/or psychedelics, if we have the willingness to ingest them) the layers of belief and neurosis that constitute the illusion of reasonableness.

Our culture is mad, completely mad, endlessly prioritizing money, power, and status over love, connection, and joy. And thank God, literally, for the opportunity not only to see beyond this madness but to feel beyond it, to know beyond it, and to know that for all the cynicism and hopelessness and unrelenting cruelty and bullshit of our corporatized and deadened political and economic systems, there are still spaces where everything can move with the mystery of the unknowable, where mystics and fairies coexist with planners and engineers as fully participating humans in the dance of civic life.

SEPTEMBER 5, 2018

Occupy Wall Street

Seven years ago, I meandered down to a little park in the Financial District to check out something called Occupy Wall Street. What I saw there, I'll never forget: hundreds of people occupying a public space, committed not just to political transformation but to each other, a genuine community built on idealism, pluralism, free expression, and love (real love, as in people taking care of each other).

I wanted to do my part. At the time, I was directing commercials, so I thought, I'll make a commercial. One of the big attacks on the movement was that nobody in it knew what they wanted. My sense was that everyone knew what they wanted, they just wanted different things, and to me, that was beautiful. So I filmed a bunch of Occupiers expressing their desires for the movement and turned it into a 30-second spot. Of all the things I've ever directed, it is hands down what I'm most proud of.

The spot went viral. It ended up on the Nightly News. A friend and I raised money and bought airtime on the O'Reilly Factor, which generated another round of attention. A mysterious man from Seattle reached out, and Occupy.com was born. I spent six months building that website with the hope of making our radical ideas more popular. Along with so many others, I gave my all to the movement. I watched it capture the world's attention and disappear, breaking our hearts.

It was seven years ago today that OWS began. Seven years since the idea of real political change went from inconceivable to sexy—until Obama swallowed it with centrism, Hillary crushed it with the establishment, and Trump borrowed its energy to advance himself. But the idea lives on and begs the question: Can we have a democracy where people's voices matter? Can we have a society that cares for every human being in it? Can we have, as Charles Eisenstein puts it, the more beautiful world our hearts know is possible—but which seems like such a dream in this consumerist simulacrum that values money above all else?

Seven years later, I am beginning to feel that the answer is no, we cannot. The forces of power are too strong and organized. And the forces of good take refuge in magical thinking, comfortable incrementalism, and tropes around doing well while doing good, as so many of us continue to fall behind.

And yet, and yet, and yet... everyone knows, or at least I believe everyone knows, somewhere deep in their being, that the radical voice is the truest one. We don't want a system where we are constantly pitted against our own needs and the needs of those we love. But we just can't believe in a better one.

That's why it's worth remembering Occupy Wall Street. We believed.

SEPTEMBER 17, 2018

Charles Eisenstein Enlightens Me

I've been in a depressive spell for the last few weeks, ostensibly brought on by money woes (that I'm embarrassed to admit have returned, despite all my previous confidence). The trap my psychology has set for me—either focus on making money and go black with sadness or follow my bliss and go broke—appears tragically inescapable. It goes so deep that four ceremonies of my beloved ayahuasca, hours communing with compassionate friends, daily mantras, and even good old fashioned giving up hasn't resolved it. Neither has any attempt to shift my mindset to gratitude or to focus on what I have. The fear of not making rent just keeps winning out.

What is going on, really?

I can touch the edges of it, touch the edges of this wound that projects itself outward as a superiority to the material world and/or a contempt for the compromises that almost everyone makes to earn a living in a capitalist economy. I see down there, at the bottom of my whole being, a little helpless baby in a crib, a baby boy who cried for hours to no avail, gave up in despair, and 38 years later needs to prove to the adult in me, no matter how much healing I do, that no one cares. I can move toward this baby, give this baby all the love I have, but it's too deep for me to heal just yet.

Some wounds are too deep for all our efforts. Some wounds simply cannot be healed until they're ready. So I helplessly reunite with the baby's original helplessness, I share my process with folks who care, I withstand well-intentioned advice about manifestation and abundance, and I pay attention to what is showing up.

Using real will, I went out to dinner the other night

and found myself across a table from Charles Eisenstein, a writer I deeply admire. A mutual friend was singing my praises, telling him how talented I was as a combination intuitive/performance artist. He was intrigued and inquired why, with my apparent gifts, I seemed so sad. I gave my best rundown about being broke. He looked at me and said, "You just don't see your value."

"No, that's not right," I responded. "I don't have a lack of self-worth. I believe I am a worthy human being."

"That's not what I'm saying. Self-worth you have. It's about value. You don't believe what you're offering is of value."

The thought made me pause. I started to see his point. It is true, even as I write these words at 3am into the Facebook void, that a part of me doesn't believe they're worth a thing (or more appropriately, a dime), that I have internalized the years of professional failure to mean that my work, my art, and my passion aren't actually valuable or else they'd be valued in proper dollars and cents. But maybe it's the opposite, if I can stand to see it. Maybe I didn't believe in the value, and so I rarely received money in return. Maybe I still don't.

At Burning Man, I took a little LSD, lay down in the temple, and closed my eyes. All these spirits started circling me, looking at me, lavishing me with attention, even taking pictures of me like paparazzi. I realized they were making fun of me. Making fun of my tendency to star in my own movie. "It's not about you," they seemed to be saying. Alright, spirits, I take your point. And I offer this episode of the David Show to those similarly lost in their own intractable problem, who may find my willingness to go there helps them feel a little bit less alone.

Deep stuff just ain't easy.

SEPTEMBER 22, 2018

My Friend Pamela Faces Death

On Tuesday, I guided my friend Pamela on a psychedelic journey. Despite a substantial dose, the effects were mild. It seemed like she was sitting on the runway, waiting for the plane to take off. "I feel," said Pam, after hours of feeling very little, "like I'm falling."

"Maybe you should fall into it," I suggested.

Pam descended. There were emotions waiting for her there, but they didn't reveal themselves. She came back up and wondered what was going on. I asked Pam to lie on the couch and put her eye mask on. I could sense the presence of a question.

"What are you afraid of?" I asked.

"Am I scared of getting stuck in purgatory?" Pam asked back, wondering if she had the right answer. But it wasn't something she needed to figure out. It was a question her body would answer in due time.

Pam has terminal cancer. Since her diagnosis, I've been making regular visits. Pam's superpower is to bring joy and positivity to every situation. My superpower is to invite whatever's going on, no matter how dark, to the surface. We're a good team.

We waited. There were tingles. "This is good," she said, bravely. "I'm uncomfortable." The tingling turned into nausea. The nausea turned into something like grief.

Tears streamed down Pam's cheeks. She hadn't cried in a while. Tears welled up in my eyes but didn't fall.

"Okay, I know how to do this," Pam said, eyes clear at the end of her trip. "When I feel safe, I let myself fall and see what happens."

"That sounds perfect."

We high-fived.

(Thank you, Pam, for letting me share this. For putting yourself out there honestly and vulnerably. You rock.)

OCTOBER 4, 2018

5-MeO-DMT

On Thursday, I smoked 5-MeO-DMT as part of a small and beautiful ceremony led by a dear friend. 5, as it's sometimes called, is the most intense of all psychedelics. It lasts only a few minutes, but it takes you far out there, or in there, or in here, depending on your worldview.

At first the smoke was harsh. I was instructed to hold, hold, hold. It hurt, until it felt nice. Soon I forgot whether I was holding or exhaling or what lungs were anyway. I lay down and, eyes closed, saw swirling red, green, and orange whirlpools of light. The sensation was of getting sucked downward. My understanding was that I was in an infinite space between dimensions.

Yet "I" was definitely still there. "I" as in the recognizable David who goes on these journeys, surveys the landscape, has revelations, and comes back to share. When, oh when, do I get to disappear? Why, in ceremony after ceremony, am I the one who's safely conscious of his own individual consciousness? Why can't my ego die?

"You're not ready," came a voice. Huh? Not ready? Yes, not ready. I bristled at the idea, but I could feel how true it was.

I have been impatient with the pace of things. As I step into a new kind of power, with gifts that flow through me, my experience is often one of frustration and loneliness. Where is everyone? I find myself wondering. What the hell is taking so long? I mean, can't we all just awaken already to the reality that this machine we're stuck in has run its course and that it's time to grow up and become our true interconnected selves?

This frustration, I learned, is a sort of projection. The truth is, I'm not ready to awaken to that idea yet, to live it out in my life, to surrender the little self that clings to his own importance within the machine, even as he seems, paradoxically, like he's working to transcend it. I'm not ready.

Another part of me protested. There are areas where I am developed. It is not only fear that allows me to hold onto my identity in psychedelic spaces; it is also a special capacity to exist in multiple dimensions at once. I won't disavow this ability just because the cosmic intelligence says otherwise. The cosmic intelligence didn't dispute me. It invited me to hold both, the child and the master, the master and the child, at the same time.

It's a wondrous place to aim at in writing, in performance, in this Facebook post. I do know things, I can channel, and I am happy to go far out there, deep into mine or another's psyche, to unearth resonant forms of truth. But I am also flailing and grasping, needing help and afraid to ask for it, spiraling into depressive spells I can't shake. Both are true. The master and the child, the child and the master.

I opened my eyes. My friend's eyes were there to meet mine. "I'm not ready," I said. He smiled. He knew me well enough to know what I meant.

Yup, I'm not ready. But I'm not alone, either.

OCTOBER 8, 2018

My Intention for My Ayahuasca Ceremony

As I've mapped the terrain of my triggers, wounds, and compartmentalizations, I have noticed one particularly elusive and excruciatingly sensitive spot lurking deep in my unconscious. It shows itself whenever I feel I must but simply cannot meet the emotional needs of a woman I'm in a relationship with. If she needs something from me but I don't feel right giving it, I split in one of two directions: either I enact the meeting of the need, going through the motions but not feeling it, or I avoid her altogether. When neither of these strategies work, I have a meltdown. You might find me collapsing onto the floor, heaving. Or going totally blank to the point of passing out. Only a few times in my life has this happened, but the underlying mechanism behind it seems to be the source of my "avoidant behavior" or fear of intimacy.

I sense I've cultivated enough compassion for myself now to return to the original trauma or traumas from whence all this came. To return to them deliberately and consciously, to relive them in my body, and to give myself, or allow the ayahuasca to give me, whatever love was withdrawn at the time. My words here are gentle, but it's possible the experience will not be: preverbal, guttural agony followed by a giving up so complete that it feels like death. All to re-associate this traumatized boy with his young heart. That is, with my heart.

I'm calm right now on my mat as twenty or so people gather in this house in Queens. I am in my element, ready to be there for myself and for whomever might need me. But if someone needs me at a moment when

I can't be there for them, I will choose myself. I'm learning.

NOVEMBER 9. 2018

The Ceremony

This past weekend, I participated in an ayahuasca retreat. As I wrote going in, my intention was to heal my absolute deepest wound, the dark spot in my unconscious that causes me to split, dissociate, or run when I'm in intimate relationships.

With the help of ayahuasca, I returned to the trauma. The fear was so intense I couldn't even feel it. It registered as numbness. I wanted to go deeper, beyond the fear, but there was nothing there, only blackness. I felt the split. The little baby was forced in two directions at once. One baby shuts down, hides out, and has been hiding ever since. This baby believes his needs will never be met. The other baby, the one who takes over, has only one way to stay alive: to please his mother. If he disappoints her, he dies.

This was my first night, this revelation. I was forced, as a baby, to choose between my mom's needs and my own. I chose both at the same time and have been living parallel lives ever since, believing they cannot be reconciled. I am so afraid of disappointing women in relationships, so deathly afraid, that I run from the possibility of doing so, or I sacrifice my own needs to not do it. It's a pattern that has hurt many people, including me.

The second night I was ready to go back into the darkness, but I was not invited there. Instead my inner child had me sit beside him. He presented as three or four years old, hiding in a jumble of logs under a pier on a beach somewhere. I held out my hand. He took it. He asked me to never leave him alone again. I couldn't promise him that, but I promised I would always be honest with him. He disappeared.

I waited, waited. The imaginary adult and the imaginary child on an imaginary beach felt more real than the bed I was lying in. Eventually, the child emerged from his fort, ashen, gaunt, and covered in soot. No one had ever cared for him. I cleaned him off. He was tentative but hopeful. I invited him to join me.

The visions stopped as the feelings began. I rubbed my fingers together like I was discovering the size of my hands. My eyes blinked rapidly. A goofy smile came over my face. And a bubbliness foreign to me but familiar to every happy child flowed through my nervous system. My little boy was trying my body on for size, seeing what it felt like. He stayed for a few minutes and left.

He returned, this time as a 14-year-old. I felt curious and rebellious. I felt the onrush of uninhibited sexual urges. I felt free. He went away again, presumably to gestate, and returned again as a 28-year-old, exuberant, bursting with excitement, ready for anything. As he left, I became very sad. I remembered that when I was 28, I was suicidal. I had no idea a shadow version of me, a joyful me, was lurking within. How sad to have lived this life instead of that one.

I wept, wept for myself, wept for the decades of slumping my shoulders and closing my heart. I thanked myself for showing up all these years when there seemed so little point, for enacting the story of the depressive artist to keep myself safe. I got up, went to the hallway, kneeled, and paid a final homage to "David." I returned to bed, mumbled "I'm not ready" about twenty times, let my arms fall listlessly to either side, and surrendered.

My heart lifted. My back arched. I could feel the other me return to my body from behind, the other 38-year-old merging with this 38-year-old. Our separate life forces fused, in a single moment, into a single being. Who was I now? I felt so... simple. My body hummed and buzzed. The voice was still in my head, the voice writing these words, but I didn't identify with that voice anymore. I was all of me.

A few days later, the fear of disappointment is still there, but the fear is like a friend. I suspect I actually did what this story suggests, as impossible as it sounds. I finished integrating all the parts of me into one person. For the first time ever, I feel whole.

NOVEMBER 15, 2018

Healing Intergenerational Trauma

On the surface, my play "Empath" is the story of how I discovered I had the ability to feel others' feelings, followed by readings with volunteers from the audience. What it's really about is the awkward journey we all take from a fixed image of self to whatever the hell wants to emerge through us. This is an invitation to be exactly who you are, exactly where you are, and to feel, with me and through me, that we are all in this together.

In the show, I tell the story of how, when I was 27, I asked my parents if I could move home for a while, because I couldn't make rent. My mom was welcoming, but my dad was not. He said, "We're not going to leave you on the streets, but whatever you have to do so that I don't have to see your face every day would be greatly appreciated." I went into my childhood bedroom, lay down on the bed, and a thick fog descended on me. It was the beginning of years-long depression.

Last night, my dad was in the audience. While I was on stage, I thought about editing this part out, right there on the spot, to protect both of us. But I went with it. The truth is, I still haven't forgiven my dad for what he did that day, but he showed up for me last night. I acknowledged my parents at the end of the play and shared how self-conscious I had been during the performance. And I expressed gratitude to my dad for coming. "I'm glad I did," he said from his seat.

My friend Joy told me that she experienced the show as a kind of ceremony. As I expose myself up there, I am showing that healing, deep healing, multi-generational healing, is not only possible but is happening in the moment. I am a work in progress, and so are you, and

"Empath" is an invitation to heal together by acknowledging it.

DECEMBER 1, 2018

It's Not About the Money

At the end of the day, it's not about the money.

So many meetings I go to, where there's inspiration and joy and love, lose their vitality when a man announces that while magic is cool and all, at the end of the day, it needs to be sustainable, i.e., it needs to make money. "How else are we going to be able to fulfill our mission?" Thus we reduce ourselves, our life force, our exuberance, to accounting. We prioritize structure over flow, and we kill the very thing that gathered us together to begin with.

May I propose this instead, to rational-minded folks who still want wonder and beauty and truth and love to flourish but who feel beholden to structures that merely want to systematize and profit from their expressions: What if you pretended for a few hours or a few days or a few weeks as if you didn't need to make money at all and watched what happened?

Maybe not now, but soon, we'll reach the stage where the hunger for authenticity—not "authenticity" in quotes but actual honesty and creative self-expression—is so strong in people that they'll buy it only if they feel it. And the way to make them feel it is to be it, truly be it, and offer it in the marketplace.

And to my friends who have money to deploy, consider investing in projects that embody what you want to see more of in the world, no matter how "sustainable" they are. Make your money an expression of your heart, so that when the teams you finance sit together brainstorming, we can follow the flow wherever it leads and not just try to return to you more of what you already have.

And women, a plea to women: women in these rooms, if you can, please stop us. Stop us men from monopolizing the conversation with our bottom lines. Please stand up for what you know to be true, that what wants to emerge in creative spaces is beyond the analytical mind's ability to process; that human beings are messy, complex, and beautiful; and that now is the time, finally, for the plotting and winning to end and the real collaboration to begin.

DECEMBER 4, 2018

The Right Person Is the One Who Is Called

When I was desperate to break through in Hollywood, I believed that all I needed to do was get in front of X person and everything would flow from there. Sometimes, I did get in front of X person, big producers, top agents, network heads. They'd like my ideas, sense my abilities, and then... nothing. My ego was so wrapped up in expressing myself on a big stage that I shrank and shrank until I was literally laying on the street, asking God for help. I was miserable and lost.

Over the last decade, I have learned—not just learned conceptually, but integrated—that my value as a human does not depend on whether I have an agent, direct a film, or make lots of money. This lesson is obvious enough, except that it flies in the face of our entire culture, and it was no small matter to come to believe it in my bones. I have also learned, when it comes to creative work, work from the heart, that there is much deeper satisfaction in having people experience it who feel drawn to it than there is in getting "the right person" to see it. The right person is the person who is called.

There are four more performances of my show "Empath." If you feel called, please follow the call and come.

DECEMBER 4, 2018

All Emotions Are Okay

In one of the readings from the show tonight, I felt something like rage emerging from deep within a 22-year-old woman. Looking at her, you'd never have guessed: high energy, bright clothes, wide-eyed, and excited to be sitting with me. But there it was, under the surface: rage.

"I sometimes feel that feeling, but I don't like to feel it, so I try not to," she said. This pattern is so pervasive that we don't realize how dangerous it is: shutting down emotions because they're negative or uncouth. To be healthy, to heal, we need a new way of engaging with ourselves.

All emotions, *all emotions*, are okay. Everything, literally everything, you're feeling is okay. If something is too much for you right now, that's okay too. Take a break and come back to it when you're ready.

We don't have a choice about what feelings are within us, no matter what anyone tells you to the contrary. If you want to find your flow, feel your feelings, and don't listen to the voices that shame and blame you for feeling them.

DECEMBER 6, 2018

If Enough of Us...

If enough of us committed ourselves to doing what our hearts called us to do, and enough of us committed ourselves to financing people who were doing what their hearts called them to do, everything else would take care of itself.

DECEMBER 17, 2018

It's Time to Wake Up

Sometimes I look around at all the sad people, desperate people, angry people, the people in subways and airplanes and on the street, and I have a strange vision: that we all stop, just stop, and suddenly all our eyes go wide, and we say to each other, with our eyes first but then with words: it doesn't need to be this way. This is all so silly. These agreements we've made with each other without realizing it, to work against our hearts, work against our planet, work against our bodies—it's enough now. We've learned what we needed to learn. And now let's start asking: What do you need, what do you really need, to thrive, to expand, to become yourself, and what do I need to do the same? And then the realization dawns on all of us at once, a revelation so obvious it feels more like remembering: what serves you serves me, what serves me serves you, and what serves you and me serves all of us. There's no need to get you to do anything for me or to get myself to do anything for you. No more guilt or shame or pressure or stress. That was how we used to do it. Now we listen, listen to ourselves and each other, and it just... works. Works better than money, better than politics, better than any system we can conceive of, because it's just us, it's our nature, and it's time.

Why not, really? It's a habit, this whole dissociated way of being. And we can shake it off. Not when we choose to, no. It's beyond choice. But when we're ready. When we're ready...

DECEMBER 18, 2018

My New Year's Resolution

My resolution is fullness. To have the experiences I'm having and to have them fully. If something is happening, allow it to happen. If something isn't happening, allow it to not happen and experience the not-happening.

The most important goals I've set in my life, goals that I dedicated my heart and soul to, I didn't achieve. I learned about powerlessness, about wanting and not getting, about the pain that comes when it feels like you can't live your purpose. But what I didn't realize was that these experiences were as valid and profound as the opposite. Not in the sense that I will "get up and try again"—enough about resilience, please—but in the sense that failure is as deep and rich an experience as success.

I still want things. I want a bigger platform. I want money to cover my needs and desires. I want a partner and children. I want a wholesale transformation of society's values. And I still have gaping holes in my psyche that I erroneously believe can be filled by reaching these goals. But I know on a deeper level that life can be rich no matter what happens to me or I make happen, and that the experience of it is all we have, anyway.

So, fullness.

And fewer desserts, too.

DECEMBER 31, 2019

The Greatest News No One Ever Shared with Me

The greatest news no one ever shared with me is that healing, deep healing, is actually possible. It is actually possible to move from anxious and fearful to calm and loving, from depressed and empty to light and joyful. The mental health establishment teaches us that it's possible only to manage our misery, never to transmute it. But it *is* possible. Not merely by changing your outer circumstances, but by reorienting around your needs as they appear, day to day, trying to be honest with yourself about what they are, and listening to your intuition about what healer or healings you're called to.

As I meander through life, having interactions with all manner of mentally unwell but perfectly normal folks, I sense such doubt, edging toward hopelessness, that anything could ever be done. Even to the point that people identify with their imbalances as permanent personality traits. But as more people do this work, more people will believe it's doable, and more spaces will open up for it, until healing centers become as commonplace as bars.

MARCH 26, 2019

A Gift from a Stranger

I walked into a healthy-ish fast food joint. The man who makes the bowls asked me how I was feeling. "So-so," I said, honestly.

"Why so-so?"

"Someone just flaked on me." I was frustrated, even sad, watching my afternoon plans disintegrate. A mild heaviness was also descending.

When I went to pay, the cashier said, "This one's on him." She pointed to the man who made my bowl.

"Really?"

"Yup!"

And just like that, the frustration melted, the heaviness lifted, and I felt a wave of gratitude. A smile came to my face.

"Thank you so, so much," I said.

"I hope you feel better."

"I already do."

Thank you to this man. Thank you to people who pause, pay attention, and give because they want to. It makes such a difference.

APRIL 3, 2019

It's Okay to Be Numb

A friend of mine asked me for some help today. She was realizing she has spent much of her life numb. She wants to soften but is having a hard time of it. I wrote back to her:

I want you to know that it's okay to numb yourself. Numbing yourself is a healthy reaction to overwhelming or intolerable circumstances. Forgive yourself for being numb.

I want you to know that being healed and whole is not better than being wounded and split. It's a journey, like aging. And each step, like each year, is as valuable as the step before it and after it.

And I want you to know that all there is to learn is to bring love to the hurt places. And if you don't have love to bring, then bring some love right there, and forgive yourself for being where you are.

You don't need to grow and change to live your destiny. Your destiny is growing and changing you already.

Love,
D

APRIL 29, 2019

How to Liberate Yourself

It's just tuning into what you're feeling, admitting the feelings into your awareness, and learning, over time, to express your feelings to yourself and to others. All the reasons why you haven't been able to feel or acknowledge or express your feelings will then appear. Working through these blocks, one at a time, is the work of liberating yourself.

MAY 20, 2019

Spiritual Growth Tip #273

Spiritual growth tip #273: Do not try to show up in all your power. You are either showing up as trying, or showing up as hiding the part of you that's scared. I recommend showing up as you are, with your desire to be in your power and your fear that you're not enough. Own that, own all of that, and you're more powerful than whoever you were trying to be.

MAY 29, 2019

What I Really Want

There are two parallel worlds.

There's the world where we know someone has genuine gifts to offer and offers them with love. We appreciate their gifts and support them on their path. Then there's the other world, the commercial world, where we don't care how genuine a person is, only how much credibility they have, how much attention they've garnered, their status, etc.

We tend to speak as if we lived in World #1. But by any concrete metric, we hire, invest, and promote projects and people of World #2. It is in this crack that I've had my heart broken again and again. I seem unable to accept the cultural gap between what is real and what is advertised as real. It hurts, keeps hurting, keeps hurting.

Some days, when it hurts the most, I wish I could dissociate and believe in the great lies that are everywhere around us. But what I really want is enough of us to join together and start valuing real things in real ways. So we can topple the false gods together.

AUGUST 3, 2019

Why I Went to Burning Man Even Though I Didn't Really Want To

At Burning Man a few weeks back, I spent an evening biking around the Playa on mushrooms with my dear friend Brundige, smiling wide and feeling joy flowing up and down my narrow frame, looking at stars and art and laughing about everything and nothing. "What would it take," Brundige asked me, "for you to feel this way all the time?"

I wanted to give the question its due. Why *don't* I feel joy all the time?

I dug around my psyche, dug around my body, looking for the trapped pain I expected to be the block, only to discover it wasn't there. It felt like the well or wells of trauma had been thoroughly drained, puked or cried out, or just plain healed. I could feel some pain still lingering about, but the pain was not holding me; I was holding it, and it was not blocking my joy anymore. So why? Why am I not living in joy? Why these sloped shoulders still? And the flat affect of my voice? And my cynical disposition? Is it habit? What?

I wasn't supposed to go to Burning Man. First, I didn't want to go that much. Second, I didn't have any money. Third, I had no ticket and no camp and a complete unwillingness to do any planning or logistics. Yet everything conspired to bring me. A free ticket appeared, courtesy of a dear friend, which set in motion a whirlwind of synchronicities that made the trip easier to take than resist. Begging the question: Why? Why was I there? If the intelligence of the universe was working to bring me, certainly it must have a good reason.

On the night the Man burned, I was pondering it all as three friends and I went from art car to art installation, alternately dancing and chatting. The joy was flowing again, that unfamiliar fluttering feeling, but as I wasn't as high, I was able to catch, just as it showed up, the resistance I have to it. A twinge of guilt, or more precisely, a sense that I'm doing something wrong, or... hurting someone? Yes, like I'm hurting someone.

Who am I hurting with my joy? I knew the answer: my dad. In the house I grew up in, joy was as rare as Monday Night Football. That is to say, never. And it wasn't just absent. It was, ever so subtly, frowned upon. Not consciously, but frowned upon nonetheless. To experience joy, let alone to express it, would feel like I was breaking my dad's unspoken rule.

Here's some backstory. My dad was born in hiding in Nazi-occupied France in 1944. After the war, his family moved to New York. Throughout his whole childhood, his parents pretended they weren't Jewish, made no mention of the relatives they'd lost in Poland, and as far as I can tell, never properly grieved. My grandmother, who died when I was 15, seemed bitter and sad for all the years I knew her. The pain ran so deep that to buy me a gift for my Bar Mitzvah was too much for her. My uncle once asked her why it was so hard to be affectionate. She responded that to show love would be like dancing on the graves of her family.

Betrayal. That's it, right there. Passed down from my grandmother to my father to me. I don't allow joy because my body believes it's a betrayal of my dead relatives. That's the block. That's why, even after all this healing, I'm not flitting about with a big smile on my face.

"I know why I came to Burning Man," I said to my friend Dorna, who had put the most effort into getting me there. We had assumed it'd be some big reason. Like I'd meet my wife. Or talk to God. Or connect with a billionaire to start the revolution. Nope. "I came to Burning Man to have fun."

SEPTEMBER 14, 2019

Why Almost No One Takes Responsibility

If there is a single universal trauma, it is around responsibility. It hurts too much for nearly everyone to say, "I made a mistake, I wish I had acted differently, and I am sorry" from a genuine place. Me too.

I think it's because we were all traumatized by our caregivers with the idea of doing something wrong. Doing something wrong meant something was wrong with us. We cannot accept fault without it meaning that we are fundamentally flawed. So we come up with a thousand ways to shirk.

If we want a world where people take responsibility for the effects of their actions, we need to make it so that people feel they will be more accepted, not less, once they own up. We need a culture that says, "No matter how awful what you've done is, you are still deserving of love."

NOVEMBER 20, 2019

The Big Lie We All Swallowed

The soft feeling of depression that has got ahold of me (once again) keeps whispering in my ear the stories of my failures. There were so many things I wanted to achieve, in the past year and in my life, that I haven't been able to, and the hurt little boy inside still doesn't know how else to tell me he needs caring for.

The lie I swallowed, that so many of us swallowed, runs very, very deep. My worth as a human, I keep telling myself, has nothing to do with my status, my bank account, or the ease with which I can make things happen. I am no less worthy than the wildly successful filmmaker I never became or the Instagram star I hear I must become to get my message out on the scale I dream of.

Lazy me, sad me, heavy me, the me who can't manifest his dreams, even the me who gives up on them—he is worthy, too, I remind myself. But it is also true that while I'm not alone in that belief, I am in the minority. Success, even belief in one's future success, brings with it so much more support, in every form, than does sadness or self-doubt or, God forbid, despair.

I am touching the bottom of this depression, and it's not that deep, I am grateful to say. I can hold it just fine and settle into it like it's an old blanket. I can bring enough love to myself, and accept enough love from others, that I can see my way out easily enough. But God, how I wish that we could all outgrow the story that put me here.

And replace it with this one: we are all glorious beings, capable of flowering and shining like the most gorgeous plants and animals of the Earth. We just need love, unconditional love, from each other. That's all.

DECEMBER 4, 2019

I Recommend Developing an Internal Sense of Self

One reason to shift from an external sense of self—I am who others perceive me to be—to an internal sense of self—I am what I feel myself to be—is that it brings deeper and more lasting satisfaction. I'm proud to say that I'm nearing the end of this particular journey, to the point where my desire to be seen as awesome is eclipsed by a much greater desire to be myself, awesome or not. It feels safe and grounded here. I recommend it.

JANUARY 14, 2020

Premium Class

As I sit down in premium class on this airplane, I feel a sense of floating. A feeling of being above and beyond. It is so difficult, even for a left-radical like me, to see this flash of class superiority as an illusion instead of something to which I am obviously entitled.

I spend a lot of time thinking about how to awaken folks with high net worths to the healing that's available if they align their money and their hearts. But I spend very little time in this cozy space of luxury, where everything whispers, "This is home." The pull of it is so strong.

Can I start, perhaps, by acknowledging the depth of the contradiction? I stand for a world built on regenerative ecological principles and the equal worth of every human being. And I revel in the fresh squeezed OJ offered to me with such delicacy in my huge seat on a transatlantic flight. I will not pretend there is no contradiction—there is, and it's deep—but I also won't pretend it's easy to find my way out. It ain't.

If you are struggling financially, I can imagine this coming across as preposterously out of touch. And if you're used to luxury, I can imagine this seeming silly and self-righteous. Quite a chasm. I don't know how to cross it. For now, I'll just gape.

FEBRUARY 16, 2020

Is This the Awakening?

I've been reading Twitter and Google News semi-obsessively, tracking the contradictions and statistics and misinformation and predictions. One of the emergent themes for me is how potentially transformational this virus is in terms of waking us up collectively. I don't want to dismiss the tragedy or the risk, but I do want to look at things from another angle.

Here are some of the lessons we're absorbing, consciously or not:

- We're interconnected, whether we like it or not. My health and my family's health depends on the sanitation of a fish market in Wuhan. It depends on the willingness of the Iranian government to shut down religious sites. It depends on hospital workers in Milan and Seoul. We were always in it together, but now it couldn't be clearer.

- Healthcare needs to be a human right if the human species is to survive and thrive. Nobody can stand up and say that a person with symptoms should have to pay for their own testing and treatment. The absurdity of this position—the fact that it puts my life and your life in danger—is apparent even to the most strident capitalists. They don't want to die, either.

- We were able, within a matter of weeks, to agree as an entire species that we are facing an existential threat, to share information, and to coordinate our responses, shutting down industries and repurposing whole swaths of our economy to the effort. This is precisely the kind of effort we need to salvage the beautiful remnants of our natural world and to address the climate crisis. Now we know it's possible.

- There has been a massive drop off in pollution in China. There has been a corresponding massive reduction in CO2 worldwide. There are big benefits to having fewer planes in the air, fewer factories whirring, fewer cars with one person in them driving to a job that could just as easily be done from home.

This virus might, *might*, be the beginning of the awakening we've been waiting for.

MARCH 3, 2020

The Dark Force Threatening to Destroy Us All

The fear around this virus is astounding. It seems to me that all the fears we cannot face—the fear that the natural world is dying, the fear that our civilization will collapse, the fear that our children and our children's children will live in an unrecognizable dystopia—these fears, unprocessed, unexpressed in the media, are driving the run on toilet paper and hand sanitizer. The machinery has given us something it's okay to be scared of, so all that fear rushes up and out, suddenly.

MARCH 6, 2020

Are We Ready?

Are enough of us ready to stand together for a new world right now?

The economy is a story. Corporations are made up. Money is imaginary. These are fictions we've invested our lives into, but they're fictions nonetheless. What is real are human beings and the need for connection. What is real are the trees and the birds and the sky and the water. We have an invitation, for those of us ready to listen, to stand for a world built on truth, not fiction.

If enough of us stand for it, it will arise. It is arising already. And the natural flow of things is here to bring it about.

MARCH 12, 2020

We're Almost There

False notes have never sounded more false. We're reaching the moment when truth and authenticity are more cherished than status and power. I can feel it.

MARCH 12, 2020

Goodbye, Bernie

One of the tragic principles of American politics, especially of the Democratic variety, is that it is never the right time to do the right thing. The right thing, whether that is universal health care, a living wage for all, an end to mass incarceration, reparations—you pick the issue, the response of the center-left is always, "We'll get to it later." Or worse: "People who demand these big changes don't get it. Just fall in line, okay?"

As Bernie Sanders takes his bow, as we say goodbye to the possibility of a president of character and conviction and heart, I am ready to mourn the dream that our political process, the sham of it, could ever meet the needs of the human beings it purports to serve. And as I mourn, I hope a new possibility dawns on us collectively: that the historic situation we are in requires a new form of government altogether, one that is not rooted in the old, patriarchal, and land-based structures of the past. We need participatory democracy, actual democracy, where people decide for themselves, for real.

It has taken me a while to step into a profoundly uncomfortable truth. But I recommend it to you, if you're ready. And if you're not ready, keep your eyes open to the possibility, because this truth is the one we will need to cross the great chasm before us together. The truth is this: the moderate voice, the measured voice, the voice proclaiming slow and steady change in light of what seems possible, is the voice of oppression, is the voice of racism, is the voice of the patriarchy. It may be the only voice you can hear, but if you listen closely, you will find cruelty in what it fails to express.

This truth is terrifying, because it demands a deeper

level of responsibility than most of us are prepared to accept. But it is also liberating, because it grants us permission to invalidate a system that runs counter to our very humanity. And once we say no, a full-throated no, we can look into the future and sense, perhaps for the first time, the emergence of a political system that is not oppositional in nature, but instead seeks to integrate, with compassion and love, the physical, emotional, and spiritual needs of every last one of us all around the world.

If this sounds utopian and naïve, I hear you. I've been hearing you for years. I heard you when I spent a month at Occupy Wall Street, risking my body for a dream. I heard you when I refused to vote for Barack Obama the second time, because he dropped billions into banks while people lost their homes. I heard you when you told me Hillary Clinton was the obvious choice. And I hear you now when you say we must rally around our only option.

But I ask you, my reasonable friends, with Trump in the White House and the world aflame, when will you hear me?

APRIL 8, 2020

We Do Not Have to Be Productive.
We Do Not Have to Be Productive.
We Do Not Have to Be Productive.

I was wrong about something.

I had thought that the great problem with our society was its obsession with money. My heart broke again and again as things I found beautiful were trodden underfoot by the cold logic of the market. I ranted about capitalism, about greed, about the inanity of a system that enshrines dollars as the ultimate form of value.

It's clear to me now, after a month in quarantine, after listening to friends, acquaintances, and clients share the pain and anxieties coming up for them, that it wasn't money that had us in its thrall all these years. It was productivity. The need to be productive is a bigger monster than greed ever was, at least in the American psyche.

I have seen multimillionaires who earned their money as honestly as it can be earned curl up in shame for not completing a to-do list. And I have seen people who don't have enough for groceries worry more about what they got done today than where their next meal is coming from. I feel it in myself, too. The pangs of guilt I feel when I remember how many emails I've left unanswered.

Even mindfulness and spiritual growth are swallowed whole by this monster. Meditation, introspection, journal writing, any form of self-care needs justifying on the grounds of being productive. When we try to escape, by setting aside unstructured time, time for things to unfold naturally, even then we justify it, quietly to ourselves, as worth doing because it serves a purpose. It's productive.

I stand in awe of this monster. It has been hiding in plain sight, gobbling up so many of our lives, laying waste to joy, curiosity, and spontaneity and offering up instead decades of grim determination and only fleeting moments of satisfaction. And for what? For the illusion of self-worth. For the illusion of mattering. For the illusion of living one's purpose.

We do not have to be productive. We do not have to be productive. We do not have to be productive. We are creatures of infinite beauty no matter what we do with our time. And if we want to live our purpose, all we have to do is live. That is enough.

APRIL 13, 2020

Afterword

You've reached the end. How was it?

I'd be curious to hear. You're welcome to email me at david@empath.nyc. And if you really liked the book, would you consider writing a review on Amazon? I'd be super grateful. Only if it flows. No pressure.

To stay in my loop, you can, of course, follow me on Facebook: www.facebook.com/davidrsauvage. You can find me on Instagram at @empathnyc. And my website is www.empath.nyc.

Oh, one last thing. In the months since I started editing this book, I gave up my New York City apartment and moved to a house in the Hudson Valley with three friends. My intention is to write another book. I'm not sure what the book is about, but I feel like it's in me, wanting to come out.

Stay tuned.

JUNE 7, 2020
ELIZAVILLE, NY

Acknowledgements

This book would not have happened without Faye Sakellardis. When you saw the book as real, you made it real. Thank you, Faye.

Avi Hakhamanesh, Heather Courtney Quinn, and Casey Schwartz all told me to write a book years ago. This isn't the book you were talking about, but it's still a book, and I am grateful you pushed me. Casey, you're like my writer-trainer. I get knocked down, stumble over to my corner; you give me water and send me back out there.

Rachel Ratliff and Diane Kelly were my first readers. You said YES. Your yesses, delivered with clarity and enthusiasm, kept me going. Otherwise, I might have been like, "Eh, whatever," and never finished.

Genevieve Bergeret, Dena Croog Cohen, and Ashley Lall got into the word-weeds with me and suggested edits that made the writing smoother. Thank you for your generosity and your fine-tooth combs. Rebecca Sauvage and Kayla Beardsley, you were the last sets of eyes. Thanks for catching those mistakes.

The cover design is by the talented Ivan Kurylenko. You nailed it. Christen Lien had excellent suggestions we incorporated. And Hannah Gaskamp did a lovely job formatting my Word document into the book you're reading now.

One last acknowledgement: Facebook. The platform gave me a way to share my thoughts and feelings that didn't even exist before it came along. As much as some of us, including me, struggle with Facebook, I hereby give the company its due. Thank you.

Made in the USA
Monee, IL
19 April 2021